Rebel Badge Book

Volume One

MERIT BADGES FOR ADULTS

52 BADGES TO HELP YOU REDISCOVER YOUR YOUTH

by Charly Lester

For Val Roberts (Brown Owl) and Sylvia Stieber (Squirrel) who inspired so much of my childhood, and supported me in so many ways.
And Nick Cooney and Sarah Theaker, who helped me make the most of my teenage years.
And for Hugo and Dudley, who have been by my side for the creation of all things Rebel.

Edition 2 - March 2023
First published October 2021

Welcome Rebels!

Hi, my name's Charly, and when I was growing up, I was a total badge geek. I was a Brownie, then a Guide, and then a Venture Scout, and I loved the buzz of ticking off tasks for a new badge, and adding another 'medal' to my stash. I left Scouting and Guiding about ten years ago, but as an adult, I've come to realise just how valuable many of the skills I learned specifically to get one of those badges ended up being. Those childhood organisations set me up for life, in a really fun and interactive way, and helped shape me as a human.

Fast-forward to 2020 and we all went into lockdown. I live alone, something which had never really been an issue before because I was always out of the house for work or socialising in the evenings. However suddenly I was in my house almost 24 hours a day, and, like most people, my world had grown a lot smaller. I found myself doing activities I hadn't enjoyed since I was a kid – knitting, cross-stitch and gardening. And when I looked online, I realised I wasn't the only one finding productive projects to focus on as uncertainty swept across the world.

Mental health issues have grown immensely in recent years – fuelled not only by the pandemic, but also by the rise of social media and constant comparison with 'perfect' lives. I lost both my parents when I was a teenager, and I have learned over the years that productivity and working my way through a 'to do' list are things which ground me and help when I'm feeling anxious or anchor-less. That was where the idea of an adult badge book came from. Why should we stop earning 'Brownie Points' aged 10 or 15? Why should learning about the stars, or camping, or making a scrapbook be things we only do as children? How can we broaden our minds and our worlds, and give something back to the environment or the community in the process?

And so the Rebel Badge Book was created! 52 badges to help you rediscover your youth! Do them with a friend, do them alone, do them with your kids, or find some fellow enthusiasts in our online community (find us on Facebook at Rebel Badge Club). And the best part? There are ACTUAL badges … once you've finished a badge syllabus, go to www.rebelbadgebook.com for details of how to claim your real life badge.

How to use this book

You can do any badge at any time, and in whichever order you like. Pick one to focus solely on, or dip in and out of a few different badges. Some badges must be completed in a set time period - for example over 3 or 6 months. Some require you to complete every clause, while others let you pick from a selection of clauses. You can earn some badges more than once - if you learn more than one language you can claim a second Linguist badge.

If you require a badge to be adapted or modified (normally for a medical reason, such as an allergy or disability) feel free to make adaptations according to your own abilities. Please keep adaptations within the 'spirit of the badge' - for example Wild Swimmer should not be completed indoors.
Badges are meant to be a personal challenge - so challenge yourself!

Timeframes are included in some badges to make you take your time, or properly focus on a particular activity. If the timescale is too short for you, feel free to extend it. Just don't rush! This book is designed to keep you busy for a few years!

If you have completed an entire badge prior to getting this book - for example the Community Service or Diarist badges - you can claim these immediately (without having to repeat the activity for another 3-6 months).

Badges are grouped into six sections, and if you complete a certain number from a section, you can also claim the corresponding Rebel Patch.

If you'd like some help along the way, head to www.rebelbadgebook.com where we'll be sharing helpful resources, and to our Rebel Badge Club on Facebook, where we have created a community of fellow rebels for inspiration and support.

YEAR PLANNER

Creative Rebel
EXPRESS YOURSELF

Artist	Dancer	Musician
Craft Part One	Designer	Photographer
Critic	Florist	Writer

Global Rebel
BE A BETTER GLOBAL CITIZEN

Activist	Entrepreneur
Animal Lover	Environmentalist
Community Service	Fundraiser
Conscious Consumer	Linguist
Emergency Helper	World Traveller

Grown Up Rebel
LEARN SOME LIFE SKILLS

Adulting	Event Planner	Investor
Baker	Gardener	Mechanic
Chef	Indoor Gardener	Money Saver
DIY	Interior Designer	

Self Aware Rebel

LET'S FOCUS ON YOU

My Brand   My Roots   My Talents

My Goals   My Style

Wellness Rebel

TAKE CARE OF YOURSELF

Apothecary   Mindfulness

Diarist   Reader

Fitness   Runner

Good Habits   Self Care

Wild Rebel

EMBRACE ADVENTURE

Adventurer   Stargazer

Camper   Survivor

Codebreaker   Wild Swimmer

Explorer   Water Sports

Outdoor Cook

MASTERPLAN

CREATIVE
REBEL

Artist

Craft Part One

Critic

Dancer

Designer

Florist

Musician

Photographer

Writer

There are lots of different ways you can express yourself creatively and this section allows you to explore a few of them. Paint a picture, make a garment, write a story, or unleash your inner critic!

Complete at least 5 of the above 9 badges to claim your Creative Rebel Patch.

ARTIST

MAKE SOMETHING BEAUTIFUL

Over a period of up to three months, complete at least four of the following projects.
Share photos of your creations with us on social media.

01
PAINT OR DRAW
A SELF PORTRAIT

02
COMPLETE A LIFE
DRAWING CLASS

03
MAKE A SCULPTURE WITH THE
MEDIUM OF YOUR CHOICE

04
MAKE A SCRAPBOOK
ABOUT AN ART PERIOD

05
PAINT A LANDSCAPE IN
OILS OR WATERCOLOURS

06
PAINT OR DRAW A PORTRAIT OF
A FAMOUS PERSON

07
SKETCH A STILL LIFE IN
PENCIL OR CHARCOAL

08
MAKE A MOSAIC WITH
MATERIALS OF YOUR OWN
CHOICE

CRAFT PART ONE

START YOUR CREATIVE JOURNEY

Over a period of up to three months, try at least five of the following activities.
You should make at least one complete item using each of the chosen crafts.
The craft does not need to be something new to you.

APPLIQUÉ	MACRAMÉ
CALLIGRAPHY	ORIGAMI
CANDLE MAKING	PAPER CUTTING
COLLAGE	PATCHWORK
CROCHET	POTTERY
CROSS-STITCH	QUILTING
FELTING	SOAP-MAKING
FLOWER PRESSING	TATTING
JEWELLERY MAKING	WEAVING
KNITTING	WOOD WHITTLING

NB - Craft Part Two appears in Volume Two of the Badge Book, together with
Advanced Crafter.

CRITIC
SPEAK YOUR MIND

Over a period of up to six months attend, read or watch at least five of the following and write a review of each one. You can review 2 of the same type of event - for example 2 plays or 2 gigs, as part of the 5. What did you love? What did you not like? How did it make you feel? Would you recommend it to a friend?

01
AN EXHIBITION

02
A COMEDY SHOW

03
A PLAY

04
A MUSICAL

05
A PANEL DISCUSSION

06
A GIG / MUSIC FESTIVAL

07
A FILM

08
A MUSIC ALBUM

DANCER

FEEL THE BEAT

Complete all 5 clauses to complete this badge.

Choose one dance form, and spend at least three months practising it regularly.

01

Research the history of this dance form, and create a scrapbook with the information you've discovered.

02

Choose three countries, and learn about their traditional national dances.
What outfits do people wear, and why?

03

Attend at least three different dance classes (each one in a different style of dance).

04

Learn and perform three dances of at least three minutes each.
We'd love if you shared videos with us.

05

DANCER

DESIGNER

Complete all 7 clauses to complete this badge.

1) Sew a garment for yourself using a shop-bought pattern. Make sure to choose appropriate fabric and accessories.

2) Create a garment for a child or baby following a shop-bought pattern. Make sure to choose appropriate fabric and accessories. (Can be sewn, knitted or crocheted)

3) Create a new garment from at least two second-hand garments. The new item should be different to its origins - e.g. a dress made from two different shirts, or a hat from a jacket and dress.

4) Design a full outfit for yourself, and make at least one of the garments.

5) Make a scrapbook about a fashion designer of your choice.

6) Design a capsule collection. Use sketches, fabric swatches, and any other images you need to bring it to life.

7) Use sewing to make a non-clothing item - for example a home furnishing, a bag or a toy. Ideally use recycled fabrics.

DESIGNER

FLORIST

BRIGHTEN UP A ROOM

Complete all 9 clauses to complete this badge.

01
TOOLS

Create a florist's toolkit and learn how to use each item properly.

02
PRINCIPLES

Learn about the seven main principles of floristry.

03
POSITION

Learn how to use floral foam and tape to hold arrangements in place.

04
PRESERVE

What substances can you add to water to preserve flowers longer?

05
VASES

Learn which shapes of vase best suit which shapes of bloom.

06
SHAPE

Explore and experiment with different shapes of flower arrangement.

07
PRACTICE

Spend at least two months practising floral arrangements.

08
BLOOMS

Experiment with a wide range of different blooms, including wild flowers.

09
PHOTOGRAPH

Keep a record of all the different arrangements you make during the course of this badge.

FLORIST

MUSICIAN

MAKE SOME MUSIC

Complete all 5 clauses to complete this badge.

01 Take time out of your week to practise an instrument for a period of at least 3 months.

02 Find a song or piece of music which you cannot currently play, and set yourself the challenge of learning to play it.

03 Practise sight reading, and play a new piece of music by sight reading.

04 Prepare a 15 minute musical programme to perform to friends or family. We'd love for you to film some of it and share it with us.

05 Create and perform a 16 bar composition. Share it with Rebel Badge Book (either publicly or privately) on social media.

MUSICIAN

PHOTOGRAPHER

CAPTURE THE BEAUTY

Over a period of three months, complete at least four of the following projects.
Share some of your photos with us on social media.

01
Take a photography course.

02
Learn how to develop your own photos.

03
Experiment with different types of photography - portrait, landscape, action, time lapse, B&W ...

04
Make a scrapbook about a particular photographer.

05
Learn about the main functions of a film camera.

06
Learn about the main functions of a digital camera.

07
Create a sequence of at least 4 related photos.

08
Create a book or exhibition of at least 20 prints.

PHOTOGRAPHER

WRITER

PUT PEN TO PAPER

Over a period of six months, regularly work on a writing project. Where appropriate finish at least a first draft. Choose one of the following projects:

01 **A NOVEL**	**02** **A NON-FICTION BOOK**
03 **A NEWSLETTER OR MAGAZINE**	**04** **A BLOG**
05 **A PLAY**	**06** **A FILM SCREENPLAY**
07 **MULTIPLE EPISODES OF A TV SHOW**	**08** **A POETRY ANTHOLOGY**

GLOBAL
REBEL

Activist

Animal Lover

Community Service

Conscious
Consumer

Emergency Helper

Entrepreneur

Environmentalist

Fundraiser

Linguist

World Traveller

This section is home to a variety of different ways you can become a better global citizen, whether that's exploring the world, volunteering in your local community, or helping to change the world.

Complete at least 6 of the above 10 badges to claim your Global Rebel Patch.

GLOBAL REBEL

MASTERPLAN

ACTIVIST

STAND UP FOR WHAT YOU BELIEVE IN

Complete all 7 clauses to complete this badge.

IDENTIFY THE CHANGE YOU WANT TO MAKE
Choose a social or political cause which is close to your heart.
Have a clear vision of the world you want to create.

01

EDUCATE YOURSELF
Read at least three books either about activism or your chosen cause,
and watch a documentary or listen to a podcast about your chosen cause.

02

IMMERSE YOURSELF
Find like-minded people - either online or at meet-ups.
Is there an organisation or charity you can become involved with?

03

SHOW UP
Attend a protest, rally, demonstration, town hall, talk or other meeting related to
your chosen cause. If you can't attend in person, how else can you support them?

04

BE COUNTED
Sign at least one related petition and use your network to rally support for it.

05

RAISE FUNDS
Run a fundraiser to support a charity or non-profit involved with your chosen
cause. If you have the means pledge a regular amount yourself.

06

ACTIVISM & THE ARTS
Study one example of how art was used to communicate a message and
create cultural change. Make a scrapbook or similar about your findings.

07

ANIMAL LOVER
ALL CREATURES GREAT & SMALL

Complete at least five of the following clauses :

01
Take full responsibility caring for
a pet for at least three months

02
If you don't own a pet, look after one which
requires round-the-clock attention (for example
a dog or cat) on at least 3 occasions.

03
Learn about three animals which
are close to extinction. What can
we do to help protect them?

04
Volunteer at an animal shelter
over a three-month period.

05
Visit a zoo, farm or
animal sanctuary.

06
Choose an animal. Make a book with facts
and pictures about the animal for a child.

07
Take an initiative which improves
conditions for wildlife - e.g. planting
bee-friendly plants

08
If you have a pet, make a proactive
change to their lifestyle to improve
their current way of life.

09
Complete a pet first aid course.

10
Volunteer to walk a dog regularly
for an elderly person.

ANIMAL LOVER

COMMUNITY SERVICE
TIME TO HELP OUT

REBEL

Volunteer on a regular basis
within your local community for
a period of at least 6 months.

CONSCIOUS CONSUMER

THINK BEFORE YOU BUY

Complete all 6 clauses to complete this badge.

Over a period of at least three months actively aim to buy as little as possible - restrict yourself to only essential purchases.
Make an active effort to find a use for things you have already bought which you may have forgotten or only part-used.

01

For a period of at least six months, only buy second-hand clothing. Buying one used item reduces its carbon, waste and water footprints by 82%

02

Explore long-term options which reduce your overall spending and wastage - for example growing your own herbs instead of buying individual packets, or using reusable sanitary products.

03

Research ways you can shop more ethically - for example only buying from independent shops, or prioritising companies run by minority groups.

04

Over a period of at least three months learn how to fix at least three different items which you would normally throw away.

05

Make at least five handmade gifts for friends and family instead of buying things.

06

EMERGENCY HELPER

BE PREPARED

Complete all 10 clauses to complete this badge.

1) Complete at least a 2 day first aid qualification which includes CPR, use of an AED, choking, anaphylaxis, severe bleeding and strokes.

2) Swim 50 metres fully clothed and demonstrate how to tow another person to safety in deep water.

3) Demonstrate how to rescue someone who is drowning without entering the water.

4) Know how to escape a car which is being submerged.

5) Know how to deal with clothing which has caught fire.

6) Know how to treat a fire which has been caused by electricity.

7) Know how to extinguish a burning pan of fat.

8) Know how to switch off the gas, electricity and water mains in your home.

9) Know how to act if you are the first to the scene of a car accident.

10) Create first aid kits for your home and car, and consider carrying a small basic kit for your handbag or backpack. What other items might be useful in case of emergency ?

EMERGENCY HELPER

ENTREPRENEUR
START-UP TIME

Complete clauses 1-6 and three tasks from Clause 7.

1) Brainstorm at least 5 different business ideas - these could be services or products. Choose your favourite idea to complete the rest of the tasks.
(Note - the exercises are theoretical, so you don't actually need to launch a business, however this could be the nudge you need to start your own company!)

2) Create a brand name, logo, and colour palette.

3) Write a basic business plan for your idea. There are lots of templates online, however some questions to consider include: Who is your target audience? Who are your competitors? What will your initial expenses be? How will you make money? How much will you charge for the product or service? How quickly are you likely to break even? Will you need any staff? Do you need to outsource any tasks? If you're making a product what is the production and distribution line? If it's a service, who will be delivering the service and how?

4) Research the brand name you chose - which trademark classes would you need to file for it? Check the TM register - are there any existing trademarks which you might be infringing?

5) Find out how you would register a limited company with Companies House (and optional - if you plan to use it - register your business name)

6) Carry out market research to find out if your idea appeals to your target audience.

7) Complete at least three of the following tasks:

- If your idea is a product, create a prototype.

- Take a class which will help you to deliver your service, or produce your product.

- Listen to at least 6 podcast episodes about entrepreneurship - they can be from the same series, or multiple different podcasts.

- Read at least one book about entrepreneurship - this could be a How To style guide, or a biography.

- If you are able to create your product, take part in a fair or market where you can sell it.

- Buy a relevant web domain for your brand and claim the relevant social media handles.

ENTREPRENEUR

ENVIRONMENTALIST

Complete Clauses 1 and 2, and six activities from Clause 3.

1) For a month, track how much rubbish you generate personally. Where practical, store the rubbish in a container, so you can understand the volume of rubbish you create each month. (Some people create less than a glass jar's worth all year!)

2) For a second month, actively reduce your waste. Find alternatives for single use plastic. Select options with less packaging, and find opportunities to re-use items. What steps did you take this month? How much did you reduce your waste?

3) Complete at least 6 of the following activities:

- Investigate eco-friendly fuel options for your house. If practical, change your energy providers so that you are using the most eco-friendly options.

- If you are a meat eater, have at least one vegetarian day per week for a month. If you are vegetarian, switch to vegan options one day per week for a month. Which meals did you cook? What substitutes did you try? Is there anything which you would eat more regularly in future?

- For a period of at least a month, actively minimise your travel carbon footprint. Walk, cycle or take public transport wherever possible.

- If you have access to a garden or allotment, plant a tree.

- Be more mindful about the amount of water you use. Switch off the tap in between tooth brushing, and when you shampoo your hair in the shower. Think of ways you can reduce your water usage or re-use 'grey' water.

- Make sure every lightbulb in your house is an energy-efficient one, and replace if not.

- If you eat seafood, make sure you are eating it from sustainable sources. Learn how to make smart seafood choices at www.FishWatch.gov

- Take part in at least one litter pick – ideally involving friends and family to increase the impact.

- Check all chemicals in your home are non-toxic – for example cleaning materials.

- Learn about 3 endangered animals. Visit a zoo or animal reserve which is working proactively towards animal protection.

- Repair something you would normally have thrown away.

- Minimise your spending for a month – buying only food and essential items.

FUNDRAISER

SUPPORT GOOD CAUSES

Complete all 6 clauses to complete this badge.

Work out what percentage of your salary you can afford to regularly donate to charity.
What charity did you choose, and why?

01

Donate your time to a good cause - over a period of three months, spend at least 24 hours volunteering.

02

Take part in a sponsored event, and where possible encourage at least two friends to join you in the challenge. Set yourself a target amount to fundraise, both individually and as a group.

03

Collect and donate food for a local food bank at least once a month for three months.

04

Research ways you can benefit charities without simply donating money - for example collecting used postage stamps.

05

Have a spring clean and donate clothes and bric-a-brac to your local charity shop.

06

LINGUIST

GET COMMUNICATING

REBEL

Languages make the world go round. Use this badge to inspire you to develop your skills in another language - whether you're starting from scratch, or brushing up on old skills. You can earn this badge multiple times in multiple languages. Please note Sign Language is a separate badge in Book Two.

Complete all 7 clauses to complete this badge.

1) Choose a foreign language to improve over the next 3 months.

2) Dedicate at least 2 hours a week to practicing your chosen language.

3) Download an app to help with your learning.

4) Have a conversation (of the relevant level for your ability) with a native speaker.

5) Choose a book, magazine or article (of the relevant level) which you will read by the end of the three months. Translate a section of it into English.

6) Cook a dish from a country where your chosen language is spoken.

7) Watch a film or TV show in your chosen language (you can keep the English subtitles on).

LINGUIST

WORLD TRAVELLER

EXPLORE THE WORLD

Complete at least six of the following clauses, including Clause 1

01
Make a list of 10 places abroad which you'd like to travel to in the next five years.

02
Make a clear plan for your next trip abroad. Where will you go? What will you do? Plan all the practical logistics.

03
Choose a country and cook at least three traditional dishes from that country.

04
Go on a trip (ideally abroad if possible) and make a visual record - this could be a video, a scrapbook, a photo album or a series of sketches.

05
Spend at least a month learning basic phrases from a new language.

06
Research three rights which we have in this country which aren't universal around the world.

07
Research the current visa and health requirements for all the locations on the list you made for Clause 1.

08
Make a guide for a tourist visiting your town about must-do or see activities, including details of how to travel there.

09
Research, and then celebrate, a festival which is celebrated in another country.

10
Try 3 different activities which are traditional to other countries.

GROWN UP
REBEL

Adulting

Baker

Chef

DIY

Event Planner

Gardener

Indoor Gardener

Interior Designer

Investor

Mechanic

Money Saver

We all have to learn life skills ... but this way you get badges for it! Improve your cooking skills, learn about money, get your tool kit at the ready or test your green fingers.

Complete at least 7 of the above 11 badges to claim your Grown Up Rebel Patch.

GROWN UP REBEL

MASTERPLAN

ADULTING

ACCEPT SOME RESPONSIBILITIES

Being an adult comes with loads of not-so-fun tasks which we all put off. This badge is designed to force you to tackle all the 'frogs' on your to do list, because the feeling when you complete them is a true weight off your shoulders!

 Complete at least six of the following adult chores, and tick them off as you go along.

	Defrost your freezer! It needs doing every six months / once the ice is over ¼ inch thick.
	Spring clean – spend two days clearing out drawers and storage areas. You might find Marie Kondo's books quite useful. Take any unwanted items to charity shops.
	If you have a car, top up the oil, water and windscreen washer fluid and check the pressure on your tyres. Keep a note of the dates when your MOT, tax and insurance need to be renewed.
	If you have a lawn, mow it regularly over a two-month period. Clean the mower and store it safely.
	Make your bed every morning. Change the sheets every week for a month, and if you have an iron, take time to iron them after drying – trust me, it makes a huge difference!

ADULTING

ACCEPT SOME RESPONSIBILITIES

✓	Tick off the chores as you complete them.
	Do the washing-up every night for at least a week, making sure not to leave anything dirty overnight.
	If you have a car, wash it at least twice during the month, and clean out the inside at least once. Polish the car at least once during the month.
	Do laundry at least once a week, iron (if needed), fold and put away clothing as soon as it is dry. Put away or wash clothes, rather than letting them pile up after wearing.
	Tidy up any 'areas of chaos' in your house – e.g. clothing chairs, piles of unopened mail, stacks of books and magazines.
	Dust skirting boards, curtain rails, tops of mirrors and ceiling corners.
	If you own a bike, pump up the tyres, clean the frame, and oil the chain.
	Choose a specific task that you know you always put off, and do it at least once a week all month.

BAKER

NO SOGGY BOTTOMS HERE!

Over a period of at least three months, bake all 9 of the following
baked goods. You might like to explore vegan and gluten-free
options for some of the tasks.

01 AT LEAST 3 TYPES OF BREAD	**02** AT LEAST 3 TYPES OF CAKE	**03** AT LEAST 3 TYPES OF BISCUIT
04 A CLASSIC PUDDING	**05** A SAVOURY PIE	**06** ECLAIRS
07 A SWEET TART	**08** A BATCH BAKE OF 12 IDENTICAL ITEMS	**09** MILLE-FEUILLE

BAKER

CHEF
COOK UP A STORM

Complete all 9 of the following tasks.

01
Over a period of 6 months actively work to improve your cooking skills.

02
Prepare at least 3 meals each week from scratch.

03
Each month experiment with a new cuisine and at least one new ingredient.

04
Master basic knife skills.

05
Cook a three-course meal from recipes you've never tried before.

06
Modify a recipe to your tastes - add or substitute at least three ingredients.

07
Cook a dinner party for at least 4 people.

08
Experiment with gluten-free or vegan cooking (if this isn't your normal diet).

09
Make a recipe book of your 20 favourite recipes.

CHEF

DIY

ROLL UP THOSE SLEEVES

REBEL

Complete all 5 clauses below:

1) Know how to turn the water, electricity, and gas supplies off to your home.

2) Change a lightbulb

3) Reset a mains circuit breaker or replace a fuse

4) Assemble a tool kit, and describe what each item is for.

5) Complete at least 2 of the following projects -

DECORATE A WALL

Prepare and then paint, paper or tile a wall.

GET SECURE

Fit security cameras or a video doorbell.

COLOUR SCHEME

Plan a new colour scheme for a room.

PUT UP SHELVES

FLAT PACK

Build an item of flat pack furniture.

UPCYCLE

Prepare and paint an item of furniture.

DIY

EVENT PLANNER
YOU'RE IN CHARGE

Over a period of up to six months,
arrange at least 3 of the following events.

01
A DINNER PARTY
For at least six people.

02
A PICNIC
For at least five people.

03
A BIRTHDAY PARTY
For a child, or a landmark adult birthday.

04
A GROUP WEEKEND
e.g. Hen Do, Stag Do, Brownie Pack Holiday

05
A STREET PARTY
Or other daytime group event for at least six people. This could be a work event.

06
A HOLIDAY
This must involve travel and accommodation logistics.

07
A CAMPING TRIP

08
A TREASURE HUNT OR WIDE GAME
For at least four people.

Event Planning Checklist

PRE-EVENT

- ◯
- ◯
- ◯
- ◯
- ◯

LAST MINUTE

- ◯
- ◯
- ◯
- ◯
- ◯

ON THE DAY

- ◯
- ◯
- ◯
- ◯

POST EVENT

- ◯
- ◯
- ◯
- ◯

EVENT PLANNER

GARDENER
GET GREEN FINGERS

Complete all 8 clauses below:

01
Cultivate an outdoor area for at least six months. This could be
- your own garden
- a friend or neighbour's garden
- an allotment
- a public area (with permission)

02
Regularly tend to your outdoor area. This might include
- mowing a lawn at least once every 2 weeks
- weeding at least twice a month
- dead-heading and pruning
- feeding plants

03
Grow at least 3 different perennial flowering plants and 3 different fruits or vegetables.

04
Grow at least 3 different plants from a seed.
Plant at least 3 types of bulb.

05
What equipment do you need to maintain your garden? How do you store this equipment to keep it safe and clean?

06
What type of soil do you have in your area? What are the advantages and. disadvantages of it? How can you improve it? Which manures and fertilisers might benefit your crops?

07
Research the reasons why bee protection is so important to our environment. Plant at least one bee-friendly plant in your garden.

08
Know basic first aid for garden-related injuries - cuts, splinters, crushing and bruising, and heat related conditions such as heatstroke and hypothermia.

INDOOR GARDENER

LET'S TALK TO SOME PLANTS

REBEL

Complete all 6 clauses below:

01
Over a period of at least 6 months keep at least 5 house plants alive! This should include at least one succulent, one cactus and one orchid.

02
Learn how much light each plant requires, and how the direction a window faces affects the light.

03
How much water does each plant need?
Which ones do you have to water more regularly?
Research the different ways to water an orchid.

04
What different products and tools can you use to promote the plants' health?

05
Know when to transplant a plant to a larger plant pot.
Transplant your cactus as it grows and monitor the impact this has on its size.

06
When your orchid loses its flowers nurture it so that it blooms a second time.

INTERIOR DESIGNER

DECORATE YOUR SPACE

Over a period of up to six months, complete
at least 4 of the following projects.

01 UPCYCLE

Repaint, repurpose or
reupholster a piece of
furniture.

02 COLOUR SCHEME

Redesign a room in your
home with a new colour
scheme. Create a visual plan.

03 WALLPAPER

Strip, prepare and paper at
least one wall.

04 FLAT PACK

Build a piece of flat-pack
furniture.

05 REARRANGE

Rearrange the furniture in one of
the rooms of your house.

06 PINTEREST

Create Pinterest boards for three
different household rooms.

07 MAKEOVER

Plan 3 different makeovers for the
same room - with a £100 budget,
£500 budget and £1000 budget.

08 FLOORBOARDS

Remove an old carpet and return a
floor to its original floorboards.
Varnish the floor.

INVESTOR

LEARN TO MAKE YOUR MONEY COUNT

Complete all 6 clauses below:

01 Actively spend time learning how stock markets work. Know the difference between stocks and shares. Why do share prices rise and fall? How do dividends work?

02 Over a 3-6 month period, track the share price of at least six different companies.

03 Research the different options you have for storing personal savings - consider bonds, stocks and shares, and different types of ISA and savings accounts.

04 What is an investment fund? Research at least three different funds and explore the cost of units for each, and how they each invest investors' money.

05 Actively research your pension options. Where possible, speak to a financial advisor - is your pension working as best as possible for your future?

06 Read at least one book about investment and listen to at least 3 podcast episodes related to investing. These could be general or about a specific topic such as crypto currency.

MECHANIC

GET YOUR MOTOR RUNNING

Complete all 6 clauses below:

Know how to open the hood of your car, check and top up oil, water and AdBlue (if necessary).

01

Know what pressure your tyres need to be kept at, how to check this and top up, and how to identify unsafe tyre tread thickness.

02

Keep an organised record of your car's service history, MOT, insurance and tax documents, and easy access details for emergency vehicle recovery.

03

Learn and, where possible, demonstrate how to change a wheel. Practice using a car jack.

04

Stock the boot of your car with an emergency kit – including a first aid kit, warm blanket and reflective clothing.

05

Know how to replace a windscreen wiper and top up windscreen fluid.

06

MECHANIC

MONEY SAVER

EVERY PENNY COUNTS

Complete all 6 clauses below:

Over a period of at least three months actively aim to buy as little as possible - restrict yourself to only essential purchases. How much money did you save in the process?

01

Review all your utility bills and regular payments - can you change to cheaper providers? Are there any direct debits or standing orders you can cancel?

02

Research different alternatives for your savings. What are the options for easy access and long-term savings? If you have any debt, could you move it to lower interest options? Are you making the most of your pension? Action any changes.

03

Find three ways you can save money in your everyday life - this might include walking or cycling instead of paying for transport, hand-making gifts and cards, or cooking more meals from scratch.

04

Over a period of at least three months learn how to fix at least three different items which you would normally throw away and replace.

05

Educate yourself about stocks, shares, crypto currency and current trends in exchange rates.

06

MONEY SAVER

MASTERPLAN

_____ _____

_____

_____

_____

_____

_____

_____

_____

_____

_____

_____

_____

_____

_____

_____

SELF AWARE
REBEL

My Brand

My Goals

My Roots

My Style

My Talents

Focus on yourself, learn about yourself, celebrate where you come from, and who you are, and plan what comes next.

Complete at least 3 of the above 5 badges to claim your Self Aware Patch.

SELF AWARE REBEL

MY BRAND

TIME FOR SOME PERSONAL BRANDING

Complete all 6 clauses below and the exercise on the next two pages.

Write a list of 10 words which you'd like other people to use when they describe you.

01

Can you translate these into 'brand values' which underpin your behaviour and decisions? Does your behaviour represent these values? Can you make any changes?

02

Look at your personal social media - are you representing your values in the things you do, say and share?

03

What are you known for among friends, family and colleagues? What would you like to be known for? What changes can you make to affect this?

04

What drives or motivates you? Write a list of plans for the next six months which tap into these drivers, and tap into your values.

05

Design a Rebel badge (or three!) which define you. What would it be called? What icon would you use? Share them with us on social media. Mine are 'Orphan Warrior', 'Rockstar Aunty' and 'Slave to my doggos'!

06

EXERCISE

As part of the My Brand badge, evaluate the following qualities. Are there any you'd like to improve on?

Self Belief

1 2 3 4 5 6 7 8 9 1 0

Positive Mental Attitude

1 2 3 4 5 6 7 8 9 1 0

Flexibility

1 2 3 4 5 6 7 8 9 1 0

Decision Making

1 2 3 4 5 6 7 8 9 1 0

Determination

1 2 3 4 5 6 7 8 9 1 0

Desire to Learn and Grow

1 2 3 4 5 6 7 8 9 1 0

MY BRAND

EXERCISE

REBEL

Now choose your own qualities and rate them.
Again, are there any you'd like to focus on improving?

....

| 1 | 2 | 3 | 4 | 5 | 6 | 7 | 8 | 9 | 1 0 |

....

| 1 | 2 | 3 | 4 | 5 | 6 | 7 | 8 | 9 | 1 0 |

....

| 1 | 2 | 3 | 4 | 5 | 6 | 7 | 8 | 9 | 1 0 |

....

| 1 | 2 | 3 | 4 | 5 | 6 | 7 | 8 | 9 | 1 0 |

....

| 1 | 2 | 3 | 4 | 5 | 6 | 7 | 8 | 9 | 1 0 |

....

| 1 | 2 | 3 | 4 | 5 | 6 | 7 | 8 | 9 | 1 0 |

MY BRAND

REBEL

MY GOALS

WHERE DO YOU WANT TO BE?

Start by identifying at least one goal for the next
6-12 months for each of the areas below.
Over the next 3 months use the worksheets to
break down your goals into actionable tasks and
make positive changes to your life.

Make a visual vision board to help inspire you.
Share a photo of your board with us.

HEALTH	CAREER	WEALTH

TRAVEL	FAMILY	LIFESTYLE

CREATIVITY	KNOWLEDGE	RELATIONSHIPS

REBEL

GOAL TRACKER

Monthly Goals :

Weekly Goals :

1

2

3

4

REBEL

GOAL TRACKER

Monthly Goals :

Weekly Goals :

1

2

3

4

REBEL

GOAL TRACKER

Monthly Goals :

Weekly Goals :

1

2

3

4

BIG GOAL ACTION PLAN

REBEL

This planner is intended to help you organise your ideas and create suitable action plans for your big goal. Categorise your main goal into sub-goals, and write the action plans for each sub-goal.

GOAL

Sub Goal 1

Sub Goal 2

Sub Goal 3

Actions

_____
_____
_____
_____
_____
_____
_____
_____
_____

Actions

_____
_____
_____
_____
_____
_____
_____
_____
_____

Actions

_____
_____
_____
_____
_____
_____
_____
_____
_____

BIG GOAL ACTION PLAN

This planner is intended to help you organise your ideas and create suitable action plans for your big goal. Categorise your main goal into sub-goals, and write the action plans for each sub-goal.

GOAL

Sub Goal 1

Sub Goal 2

Sub Goal 3

Actions	Actions	Actions
_____	_____	_____
_____	_____	_____
_____	_____	_____
_____	_____	_____
_____	_____	_____
_____	_____	_____
_____	_____	_____
_____	_____	_____
_____	_____	_____

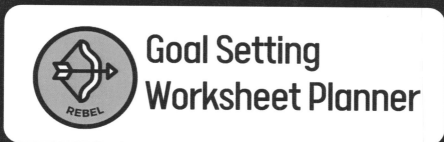

Goal Setting Worksheet Planner

01

Goal :

Steps :

02

Goal :

Steps :

03

Goal :

Steps :

Goal Setting
Worksheet Planner

REBEL

04

Goal :

Steps :

05

Goal :

Steps :

06

Goal :

Steps :

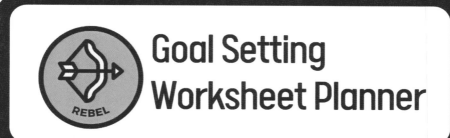

Goal Setting Worksheet Planner

07

Goal :

Steps :

08

Goal :

Steps :

09

Goal :

Steps :

MY ROOTS

EXPLORE YOUR FAMILY TREE

REBEL

Spend at least six months researching your family tree. Where possible, source images of relatives and record interviews with family members for posterity. Present your findings in a way which is accessible to your wider family.

MY STYLE

Time to review and update your wardrobe!

REBEL

01 Every day for a month, take a photo of your outfit. Which is your favourite? How did it make you feel? And your least favourite?

02 What percentage of your wardrobe do you currently wear? What colours, items, styles and silhouettes did you wear most often?

03 How would you describe your style in words? How does it make you feel? How would you like it to make you feel? What messages do your current looks share with others?

04 Make a collage, scrapbook or Pinterest board of outfits you love. Get inspiration from magazines, blogs and TV shows.

05 Review your current wardrobe - how could you create some of the outfits you love with existing clothes? What do you need to add? Decide on up to 5 items for a wish list.

06 Now return to your wardrobe - are there any items you haven't worn for over a year, which don't fit your ideal aesthetic? Donate these to charity.

MY TALENTS

BE YOUR OWN BIGGEST FAN

Write a list of 5 things you're good at, and 5 things you'd like to improve on.

01

Choose one of your 5 talents, and find a way to use it to help others. This could be through teaching, coaching, or volunteering.

02

Choose another of your 5 talents, and find a way to share it - e.g. giving a gift, a demonstration, a performance or publishing it.

03

Choose one of the 5 things you'd like to improve on, and over a 3 month period give yourself SMART goals to work pursue.

04

Choose one of the 5 things on your improvement list, and take a class, read a book or download an app which will help you with that skill.

05

Think about your friends and family. What are their skills and talents? Actively be more vocal praising others for their skills.

06

MY TALENTS

WELLNESS
REBEL

Apothecary

Diarist

Fitness

Good Habits

Mindfulness

Reader

Runner

Self Care

This section will help you spend more time focussing on yourself, your health and your wellness. Whether it's fitness, me-time, or chilled out hobbies, explore what wellness means to you.

Complete at least 5 of the above 8 badges to claim your Wellness Rebel Patch.

WELLNESS REBEL

MASTERPLAN

APOTHECARY

MIX UP A STORM

Make at least 5 of the following products from scratch -
experiment with fragrances and ingredients.
Share photos with us!

01
A FACE MASK

02
MOISTURISER

03
LIP BALM

04
TONER

05
PERFUME

06
EXFOLIATOR

07
SHOWER GEL

08
SHAMPOO

DIARIST

HOW DO YOU FEEL?

REBEL

Over a period of six months, write a journal at least four times per week. You can decide whether you keep a gratitude journal, a bullet journal, a 'one line a day' diary, or a more detailed account. If you've never kept a journal before and don't know what works best for you, feel free to experiment over the six months.

FITNESS

GET ACTIVE!

REBEL

Set yourself a target number of days per week you wish to exercise - for example 3, 4 or 5. Multiply this number by 12. Over a three month period, complete that number of days of exercise - don't panic if you have a bad week or two, you can always catch up later. Depending on your current level of fitness, an exercise session might be a 30 or 60 minute walk, a bike ride, 30 laps of a swimming pool, a 5k run, a spin class, or an aerobics class. Be honest with yourself, and try to challenge yourself a bit. Use this three months to try some new classes or activities. Remember - any fitness activity counts as another day ticked off!

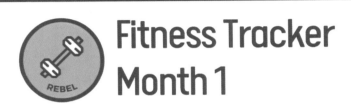

Fitness Tracker
Month 1

Month:

Target Number of Days :

Use the tracker below to record every day of exercise you complete this month. You may wish to count the days as you go along, use crosses when you exercise, or add dates to the days.

MONTHLY GOALS

MON	TUE	WED	THU	FRI	SAT	SUN

Fitness Tracker
Month 2

Month:

Target Number of Days :

Use the tracker below to record every day of exercise you complete this month. You may wish to count the days as you go along, use crosses when you exercise, or add dates to the days.

MONTHLY GOALS

MON	TUE	WED	THU	FRI	SAT	SUN

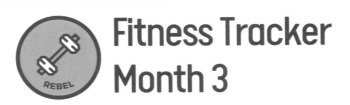

Fitness Tracker
Month 3

Month:

Target Number of Days :

Use the tracker below to record every day of exercise you complete this month. You may wish to count the days as you go along, use crosses when you exercise, or add dates to the days.

MONTHLY GOALS

MON	TUE	WED	THU	FRI	SAT	SUN

GOOD HABITS

GET INTO THE SWING OF THINGS

REBEL

1) Decide on a positive change you wish to make in 4 areas of your life - life admin, health and fitness, household chores and self care. You could use the Adulting, Runner, Fitness, Mindfulness and Self Care badges for inspiration (and might want to do some of them at the same time).

2) Over a period of at least 90 days, create positive habits for yourself, by regularly making the 4 chosen changes to your life.

3) Read or listen to a book about habit-making to help with your goal. My personal suggestion is 'The Power of Habit'.

Monthly Log

LIFE ADMIN HABIT:

HEALTH AND FITNESS HABIT:

HOUSEHOLD HABIT:

SELF CARE HABIT:

TRACKER

MON	TUE	WED	THU	FRI	SAT	SUN

Monthly Log

LIFE ADMIN HABIT:

HEALTH AND FITNESS HABIT:

HOUSEHOLD HABIT:

SELF CARE HABIT:

TRACKER

MON	TUE	WED	THU	FRI	SAT	SUN

Monthly Log

LIFE ADMIN HABIT:

HEALTH AND FITNESS HABIT:

HOUSEHOLD HABIT:

SELF CARE HABIT:

TRACKER

MON	TUE	WED	THU	FRI	SAT	SUN

MINDFULNESS

BE PRESENT IN THE MOMENT

Complete all 5 clauses below:

Over a period of 3 months take time out of your day to meditate regularly. You may find an app helps with this. **01**

Try at least three different forms of yoga. Is there one which works best for you? Take classes at different times of day to work out when you get the most benefit. **02**

Keep a gratitude journal for at least a month. Every day make a note of 5 things which you are grateful for - you may wish to start or end your day in this way depending on your routine. **03**

At least once a week, over your three month period, make time for a creative activity which quietens your mind - this might be drawing, painting, knitting ... **04**

At least once a week do something which helps you to indulge your body - this might be a long bath, a massage or a skin care regime. You may wish to vary the 'me time' activity each week. **05**

READER
PAGE BY PAGE

Complete all 5 clauses below:

01 Over a period of three months read at least six books. If you want more of a challenge, aim to read a book a week.

02 Include at least one fiction, one biography and one non-fiction book in your list.

03 Write a review of one of the books.

04 Read a review of one of the other books, and critique it. Which points do you agree with, and which points do you disagree with?

05 Take part in a Book Club. If you're not already a member of one, recruit at least two friends to read the same book. Meet up (in real life or virtually) to discuss your thoughts on the book.

READER

RUNNER

ONE STEP AT A TIME

REBEL

Complete all 5 clauses below:

Over a period of 2 months, run or walk 5km at least once a week (ideally running more and more of the 5km each week). You may find your local parkrun or the Couch to 5k app may help with motivation.

01

Depending on your level of experience, sign up to a 10k, Half Marathon, Marathon or Ultra Marathon and follow a training plan to train for the race over at least 3 months. Complete the race.

02

Research different nutrition options for your race. Can you change what you eat during training, in the days running up to a race, during a race, or after a race? Which products work for you? Which don't?

03

Research future challenges - are there any longer runs, triathlons or run-swims which appeal to you?

04

Are there any changes you need to make to your kit? What works well? What doesn't?

05

SELF CARE
BE YOUR OWN BEST FRIEND

Self care means different things to different people, so pick at least 4 of the following things, and make time to do them regularly over a 3 month period.

01
BATHTIME
Find the perfect bath recipe! Experiment with different oils, salts, bubbles, candles, music etc.

02
SLEEP
Work out your optimum amount of nightly sleep, and aim to get it at least 5 times a week.

03
BEDTIME
Experiment with your bedtime routine - scents, white noise, temperature, lighting, screentime etc.

04
DIET
Make a positive change to your diet - for example cutting out meat for 3 months.

05
SCREEN TIME
Make an active effort to limit your screen time or time spent on social media.

06
PAMPER
Regularly schedule in beauty treatments - such as massages or pedicures, or make time to give yourself home treatments.

07
ALCOHOL
Give up alcohol for three months.

08
YOUR CHOICE
Focus on your own area of self care - this might be meditation, buying yourself flowers, reading more, exercising more ....

WILD
REBEL

Adventurer

Camper

Codebreaker

Explorer

Outdoor Cook

Stargazer

Survivor

Wild Swimmer

Water Sports

This section will help you discover, regain or grow your sense of adventure! The badges are designed to help you make the most of the outdoors in a variety of different ways.

Complete at least 5 of the above 9 badges to claim your Wild Rebel Patch.

WILD REBEL

MASTERPLAN

_____

_____

_____

_____

_____

_____

_____

_____

_____

_____

_____

_____

_____

_____

_____

ADVENTURER

MAKE THE MOST OF THE OUTDOORS

Over a period of up to three months, try at least five of the following activities.

If you complete a different set of five, you can claim another badge.

Make sure you take lots of photos ... you'll want to remember this badge!

ABSEILING

ARCHERY

AXE THROWING

BOULDERING / ROCK CLIMBING

BUNGEE JUMPING

CANYONING

COASTEERING

CROSSBOW SHOOTING

FENCING

FLYING TRAPEZE

GO-KARTING

HANG GLIDING

HIGH ROPES / TREE CLIMBING

HORSE RIDING

HOT AIR BALLOONING

INDOOR SKY DIVING

MOUNTAIN BIKING

PARAGLIDING

PARKOUR

RIFLE SHOOTING

SKATEBOARDING

SKIING

SKYDIVING

QUAD BIKING

ZIPLINING

ZORBING

YOUR CHOICE

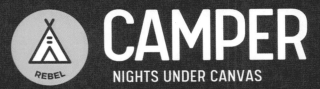

CAMPER
NIGHTS UNDER CANVAS

Complete all 10 clauses below:

Spend at least 3 consecutive nights under canvas
This could be at a festival, on holiday or in your garden.
Please do not camp solo for this badge.

01

Pitch and strike the tent
Know the functions of the poles, pegs, ropes and
fly sheet.

02

Keep your belongings safe and dry
Air out bedding, prevent items from getting wet
overnight, and think carefully about storage options.

03

Design the menu for the trip
Think carefully about food storage when you don't
have electricity.

04

Kit out your camp kitchen
Make sure to take all the equipment you'll need to
cook everything from your menu.

05

CAMPER

Cook at least 4 meals outdoors

Use either a camp stove or an open fire. Make sure to take all necessary safety precautions.

06

Leave minimal trace

How can you keep your camp as environmentally friendly as possible? Take all necessary steps.

07

Know how to treat camp injuries

Learn basic first aid for cuts, stings, burns, scalds, sprains, splinters and serious bleeding.

08

Prepare a first aid kit for your trip

Take care with expiry dates. Be aware of any allergies or medical issues. Make a note of where the nearest emergency help is – A&E department, Coastguard etc.

09

Take part in 3 outdoor activities during camp

These could include a campfire, adventurous activities, a treasure hunt, camp gadget building, orienteering, or outdoor crafts.

10

CAMPER

CODEBREAKER
EXERCISE YOUR MIND

I've always been a huge escape room fan - they remind me of the game shows I watched as a child, and I enjoy being transported to another world for an hour. I love the way they allow you to have a proper adventure indoors, or even from your own sofa if you're doing a virtual escape room. Broaden your horizons and explore the unknown with this badge.

Complete at least 5 of the following tasks:

1) Learn Morse Code or Semaphore.
2) Learn the phonetic alphabet.
3) Over a period of up to three months, visit at least three different themed escape rooms. (You can do this virtually or in person) Which was the best? What did you enjoy? What didn't you enjoy?
4) Research the following ciphers - classic substitution, Caesar cipher, homophonic substitution, Vigenère cipher, book cipher, Playfair cipher, ADFGVX cipher, Enigma cipher.
5) Learn three practical ways to hide a message.
6) Make a code wheel.
7) Either take part in a treasure hunt, or set one for other people.
8) Learn about the history of the codebreaking, and if possible visit a museum related to code breaking – for example Bletchley Park or Imperial War Museum.
9) If you were to create your own escape room, what theme would you choose? What kinds of activities would you include in it? Plan at least three puzzles.
10) Read a 'choose your own adventure' book or complete a puzzle book or puzzle game.

NOTES :

_____

_____

_____

_____

_____

_____

_____

EXPLORER

NAVIGATE YOUR OWN WAY

This badge is designed to help you gain confidence trekking and exploring. You can decide to go as far afield as you like to complete the badge, and you're the one setting the limits for yourself, just make sure to challenge yourself. For safety, never trek alone, and if you are somewhere remote, it's advisable to stay in groups of at least three so someone can always go for help if one of you has an accident. Apps such as What Three Words and Find My Phone can be really useful for staying safe whilst exploring.

Complete all the following clauses:

1) Learn to navigate using an Ordnance Survey Map. Be able to identify what the different symbols mean, and work out distances and differences in heights between two points on a map.

2) Set a map using a compass.

3) Over a period of three months, hike outdoors regularly, and keep a log of the walks, including date, distance, location and weather.

4) What hiking gear do you find most practical and comfortable? What items do you bring with you on short hikes. What do you pack for longer ones?

5) Plot a route of at least 10 miles on a map and walk or cycle it.

6) Plan a challenging day trip with at least two other friends - trek at least 20 miles, climb a mountain, kayak at least 10 miles, or cycle at least 40 miles.

Where did you go?
Who did you go with?
What did you do?
What was the best part?
What did you learn?

7) Pack a bag for the day trip including lunch, snacks, safety equipment and anything else you need to complete the day trip. What did you pack?

8) Plan an overnight adventure trip, where you spend at least one night in a tent.

Date:
Where did you go?
Who did you go with?
What did you do?
What was the best part?
What did you learn?

9) Plan an overnight stay somewhere you've never been before. It should be at least one night but could be more, alone or with friends, however, you should be the organiser. Plan and arrange accommodation, transport, food and drink, and at least two activities.

Date:
Where did you go?
Who did you go with?
What did you do?

What was the best part?
What did you learn?

10) Take part in a challenging organised event which includes hiking or long-distance cycling. This could be a race such as Race to the Stones, a charity event, such as the Moonwalk, or a cycling sportive. You set the limits - whether it's climbing Mount Kilimanjaro, cycling from Land's End to John O'Groats, or walking a local Half Marathon, find something which is a genuine challenge to you, and which you will be proud to complete. Send us a photo from the finish line of this challenge!

OUTDOOR COOK
STRIKE UP THE FIRE

REBEL

Master the art of outdoor cooking, and become everyone's favourite person on a campsite in the process! You can complete this badge in your back garden, or on a designated campsite - just make sure you have permission to light a fire, or have an open flame, and that you take all necessary safety precautions - for example, always have a fire bucket to hand. Complete all 8 clauses.

01. Cook a meal on an open wood fire.

02. Collect and stack suitable firewood. What safety precautions do you need to take when lighting a fire?

03. Cook a meal on a portable stove

04. What safety precautions do you need to take with your stove? How do you refuel the stove?

05. Cook a meal on a barbecue.

06. How would you store ingredients outside? How long can you safely store each ingredient without electricity? How can you keep food cool, dry and away from animals?

07. Make a pocket first aid kit. Know how to treat cuts, burns and scalds.

08. Make a menu book of at least 10 dishes which you can cook outside.

One of the above meals should be for 2 people, one for 4 people, and one for 6 or more people.

STARGAZER

LOOK TO THE SKY

Complete all 8 clauses below:

01
LOGBOOK

Over a period of two months regularly observe the night sky, at least twice a week. Keep a logbook of the constellations, moon and any planets you see.

02
UPCOMING EVENTS

Research any major astronomical events happening in the next few months.

03
SOLAR SYSTEM

Learn about the planets - their relative size and positions. Build a model of the Solar system. Send us a photo!

04
THE MOON

Learn about the phases of the Moon, and the effect it has on the Earth.

05
THE STARS

Draw at least 10 constellations. Make clear which are visible in the Northern Hemisphere or the Southern Hemisphere.

06
HISTORY

Research the history of space exploration and write a timeline of major occurrences from the 1950s onwards.

07
COMPASS DIRECTIONS

Understand how to work out compass directions from the night sky.

08
VISIT

Visit a planetarium, observatory or science centre.

STARGAZER

This badge is dedicated to Bob Lester.

SURVIVOR
FEND FOR YOURSELF
REBEL

Complete all 10 clauses below:

1) Build an emergency shelter and (optional, depending on the time of year) sleep in it!

2) Research 4 different ways to find water in a survival situation.

3) Know when and why water needs to be purified and how to do so.

4) Identify three edible and three inedible plants in your local area.

5) How would you survive if you fell into cold water, fully clothed? If possible, practice treading water fully clothed in a swimming pool.

6) Find North with and without a compass (by day and night).

7) Light a fire without matches.

8) Describe how to escape a car which is sinking under water.

9) How do you prevent and treat the effects of extreme heat (dehydration and sunstroke) and extreme cold (hypothermia)?

10) Learn CPR, including the differences after suspected drowning, and the difference between adults, infants and babies.

WATER SPORTS
GET IN THE SPLASH ZONE!

Push yourself out of your comfort zone with this varied list of activities. Explore some local rivers or lakes, head to the coast, or add some adventure to your next holiday.

Over a period of up to three months, try at least five of the following activities.

CANOEING	SAILING
CANOE POLO	SCUBA DIVING
DIVING	SNORKELLING
DRAGON BOAT RACING	STAND UP PADDLEBOARDING
INFLATABLE OBSTACLE COURSE	SURFING
JETSKIING	SYNCHRONISED SWIMMING
KAYAKING	WAKEBOARDING
KITE SURFING	WATER POLO
LIFEGUARD TRAINING	WATERSKIING
PARASAILING	WHITE WATER RAFTING
RAFT BUILDING	WINDSURFING
ROWING	

If you complete a second set of five activities you may claim a second badge.

WILD SWIMMER

TIME TO GET WET!

Complete all 10 clauses below:

1) Over a period of three months, swim in open water at least once a week. If you are swimming alone, please do so in a designated open water lake.

2) During the three-month period, swim in at least three different open water venues.

3) Keep a record of water temperature, who you swam with, time, weather conditions and how far you swam.

4) Learn how to administer CPR to a victim of drowning. How is this different to other forms of CPR?

5) What equipment do you need to swim in cold water? How can you stay as visible as possible to others while open water swimming?

6) How should you store a neoprene wetsuit? How do you fix small holes? How do you prevent creating holes in a wetsuit?

7) Describe the differences between a swimming wetsuit and a surfing wetsuit. How is a swimming wetsuit specifically designed for swimming?

8) Describe how a non-swimmer, weak swimmer and injured swimmer look in the water.

9) Learn how to tow someone in the water.

10) Take part in a 'fun' open water swimming activity – this could be a night swim, a swim-run event, a triathlon, a swimming race, a New Year's Day swim, coasteering, canyoning, or an inflatable water park.

BADGE TRACKER

CROSS OFF EACH BADGE AS YOU EARN IT OR ADD STICKERS

BADGE TRACKER

CROSS OFF EACH BADGE AS YOU EARN IT OR ADD STICKERS

Over the past year since the first edition of Rebel Badge Book was published, the accompanying Facebook group 'Rebel Badge Club' has grown in size, and so have the ideas and opportunities which have sprung from the community.

In addition to this first badge book, and the 52 badges included in it, there are now a whole host of other ways in which you can get involved with Rebel Badge Club.

Volume Two of Rebel Badge Book was published in November 2023.
It includes 52 more badges.
Badges from Volume Two can be used towards the Section patches.

Once you've completed all seven of the Section Patches (Creative, Global, Grown Up, Self Aware, Wellness and Wild) you are eligible to claim the Ultimate Rebel badge.

At the request of Rebels in the Facebook Group, I created a bespoke dotted journal and workbook - Rebel Badge Journal. There is a second volume to accompany Volume Two of Rebel Badge Book.

Struggling to work out where to start with the badges? Every three months there is a new 'Quarterly Challenge Badge' in the Facebook Group, which you can claim once you have completed the relevant merit badges. Previous Challenges have included Carpe Diem, Be Kind, and a New Year's Challenge badge.

Monthly challenge badges have also been introduced to the Group. Easier than merit badges, these one-off badges span a wide range of activities - from Scavenger Hunts, to charitable work, to Christmas and Halloween seasonal badges.

The Maverick Awards are a set of long term, assessed Awards, designed to challenge Rebels for six to eighteen months. Rebels start the Awards with Bronze, and can then progress to Silver, and later Gold, after completing each stage of the Awards.

The Bronze Maverick includes five sections - My Community, My Beliefs, My Challenge, My Adventure and My Skills. Some sections require you to present projects, some need a six month record of activities, and the Award will be assessed over Zoom once you finish.

The Rebel Council is a steering committee for Rebel Badge Club. Members pay a monthly subscription, and have membership numbers and exclusive badges. The Council is used to debate future badges and challenges, and develop ideas of how Rebel Badge Club evolves. Members receive earlybird access to all new Rebel products, and discounts on certain items of stash.

Spoonie Rebels is a Facebook group for disabled and neurodiverse Rebels. Created by Rebels, it is specifically designed for Spoonie Rebels to discuss badge adaptation for medical reasons in a safe, understanding space.

The Rebel Cup is a fun game in the Facebook group, designed to incentivise you to finish badges! Choose your Patrol, and score points for them each month in a variety of fun and silly ways. Yes, there are special badges you can collect along the way!

Live Rebel events have begun. August 2023 sees the first Rebel Summer Camp in Blackwell, England, and official Big Rebel Meet Ups will be held in various cities and countries around the world. Rebels have been encouraged to create local 'Rebellions' to meet up with Rebels in their local area - links to these groups can be found in the main Facebook group.

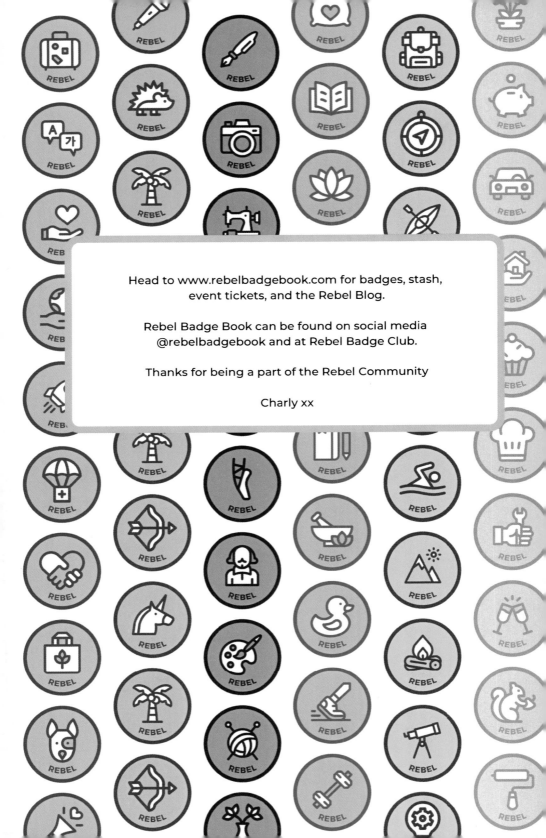

Head to www.rebelbadgebook.com for badges, stash, event tickets, and the Rebel Blog.

Rebel Badge Book can be found on social media @rebelbadgebook and at Rebel Badge Club.

Thanks for being a part of the Rebel Community

Charly xx